THE 2000 YEAR JOURNEY OF CHURCH GROWTH

RAY JAMES

PUBLISHED by PARABLES
Earthly Stories with a Heavenly Meaning

The 2,000 Year Journey of Church Growth
Ray James

Published By Parables
August, 2020

All Rights Reserved. No part of this book may be reproduced or utilized in any form or by any means, electronic or mechanical, including photocopying, recording, or by any information storage and retrieval system, without permission in writing from the author.

    ISBN **978-1-951497-78-1**
    Printed in the United States of America

Readers should be aware that Internet Web sites offered as citations and/or sources for further information may have been changed or disappeared between the time this was written and the time it is read.

THE 2000 YEAR JOURNEY OF CHURCH GROWTH

RAY JAMES

PUBLISHED by PARABLES
Earthly Stories with a Heavenly Meaning

Ray James

About the Author

Ray James is an ordained minister and has pastored in Illinois, Pennsylvania, Maryland, and Virginia. He has a Bachelor's Degree in Theology, a Master's Degree in Pastoral Ministry, and a Doctorate in Ministry. Dr. James is a pastor, author, teacher, conference speaker, and international preacher who has travelled to over 40 countries on five continents, and across 49 states in the United States. He and his wife, Linda, reside in North Carolina. They have two adult children, eight grandchildren, and six great-grandchildren.

Ray James

The 2,000 Year Journey of Church Growth

TABLE OF CONTENTS

Prologue
5

Chapter One
Origin of the Church
9

Chapter Two
The Early Years
19

Chapter Three
The Latter Years
25

Ray James

Chapter Four
The Next Church
31

Chapter Five
A Post-Pandemic Word
55

Chapter Six
Closing Thoughts
59

Prologue

At the time of this writing nearly every nation of the world is engaged in the Coronavirus Pandemic of Covid-19. Some countries have remained in a total quarantined 'lock-down', and some countries have greatly loosened restrictions and are resuming a 'business as usual' stance; and some have flip-flopped back and forth as loosening of restrictions has proven to not be successful.

Much turmoil has been caused to our nation, and, in return, to our churches. Some have suggested the Covid-19 Pandemic was intentionally caused very soon after the signing of the trade agreement between China and the United States, because it would release China from major restrictive conditions to the agreement. Others believe it was a political ploy to hurt our economy and cause President Donald Trump to lose the upcoming election. Regrettably, the turmoil caused by all of this, has not only hurt our economy, it has also hurt our everyday way of life including our opportunities to corporately worship God in our church buildings.

While those who are much more intelligent than I am try to figure this out, I will simply concede that I don't know. What I do know is that Jesus Christ is still sitting on His heavenly throne at the right hand of our Father, and they are in total and perfect control of all things, and have a purpose for allowing this to happen; the primary purpose, I believe, is His church. During this pandemic, we have watched as some have tried to defy the orders of those over them and continue to gather to worship in their church's buildings. We have also watched as many of those people were arrested and fined.

For several Constitutional and political reasons those people chose to not obey the directives of their leaders, quoting the Words of Jesus (Matthew 16:18), that "[He] will build His church and the gates of hell will not prevail against it."

In the United States, several states are transitioning to a Phase-2 position of reopening businesses in an effort to restore our economy to pre-pandemic levels. Most of these states have seen enormous increases in the number of people infected, hospitalized, and in deaths, which has caused their governors to return to the practices of wearing face masks and social distancing.

At one point, our churches were forced to close their doors and become creative in methods to conduct weekly services, from empty sanctuaries via livestreaming on their web sites, on Facebook, and other venues. Some churches even experimented with drive-in services where families sat in their cars facing a make-shift platform for the worship leader, musicians, and pastor.

Over these past couple of months, much discussion has been made regarding what the church will look like at the end of this pandemic. Will the church go back to the way it was? Will changes need to be made, and, if so, what will those changes be?

As we emerge from the restrictions caused by the Coronavirus, and ponder the direction of any changes to be made in our churches, this would be an excellent time to readdress the words of Jesus when He said, "I will build *my* church" (emphasis added).

What was He saying to Peter, and the other disciples, and what is He saying to us today, as we reexamine His church?

Christ's church is not a building in which people worship Him, but rather, His church is comprised of the people from every racial, cultural, and ethnic background who have accepted Him, Jesus Christ, as their Lord and Savior; placing their faith in the redeeming sacrifice He made for them through His shed blood on the cross of Calvary.

Certainly there will be some changes made, so join me in an historical and scriptural journey from that warm summer day, believed to have been in August of 32 C.E. on the coasts of Caesarea Philippi, to the post-pandemic days ahead.

Ray James

Chapter One

Origin of the Church

Matthew 16:13-20 says, "When Jesus came into the coasts of Caesarea Philippi, he asked his disciples, saying, 'Whom do men say that I the Son of Man am?' And they said, 'Some say that thou art John the Baptist, some Elias; and others, Jeremias, or one of the prophets.' He saith unto them, 'But whom say ye that I am?' And Simon Peter answered and said, 'Thou art the Christ, the Son of the living God.' And Jesus answered and said unto him, 'Blessed art thou Simon Barjona; for flesh and blood hath not revealed it unto thee, but my Father which is in heaven. And I say also unto thee, That thou art Peter, and upon this rock I will build my church; and the gates of hell shall not prevail against it. And I will give unto thee the keys of the kingdom of heaven: and whatsoever thou shalt bind on earth shall be bound in heaven: and whatsoever thou shalt loose on earth shall be loosed in heaven.' Then charged he his disciples that they should tell no man that he was Jesus the Christ."

To His disciples, His true identity was finally revealed, and the foundation of His church was laid.

When Jesus said, "Thou art Peter" the Greek word used here for Peter would have been "Petrus"; and when Jesus said, "…and upon this rock…", the translated Greek word for "rock" used was "petra".

(Petra defined as "a rock", and Petrus defined as "a piece of rock" or "stone".)

The interpretation of this being: that Jesus Christ is the Rock on which the church would be built; and that Peter's confession of faith in Jesus Christ as the Son of God, places Peter as a piece of that rock.

Several times in the Psalms, and in 2 Samuel 22:32, God is referred to as "a rock", and in Isaiah 28:16 (700 years earlier), God told the Prophet Isaiah, "Behold I lay in Zion for a foundation a stone, a tried stone, a precious corner stone, a sure foundation…". Although His disciples could not yet fully understand the extent of this "foundation", there was no doubt that Jesus the Christ was *that* foundation, and that Peter's confession of faith in Jesus as the Son of the living God would make him a part of that foundation.

The foundation was being laid for what we know today to be His church, but what functions of His church would this foundation support?

For a timeline, let me begin with the end of Jesus' ministry. Matthew 27:50-52a says, "And when Jesus had cried out again in a loud voice, he gave up his spirit. At that moment the curtain of the temple was torn in two from top to bottom. The earth shook, the rocks split and the tombs broke open…". (NIV)

An analysis of earthquake activity in the region by the Supersonic Geophysical and the German Research Center for Geosciences have concluded that Friday, April 3, 33 C.E. is the best calculated date of the crucifixion of Jesus Christ, when data about the revised Jewish calendar and when other astronomical calculations are considered.

Now, let's focus on the teachings of Jesus from the Matthew chapter 16 conversation with His disciples in mid-year 30 C.E. through April 3, 33 C.E., to catalog some of the functions of His church for which His foundation was laid.

In no particular order, here are some of the functions Jesus desired for His church:

1. In Mark 16:15, Jesus said, "And then he told them, 'You are to go into all the world and preach the Good News to everyone, everywhere'". (LB) The Good News He was speaking of was the arrival of their long-awaited Messiah, referring to Himself, and the coming of the Kingdom of God, God's messianic kingdom, ruled by the Redeemer of God's people who would accept Him as their Lord and Savior. That gospel was to be shared with "everyone, everywhere".

   Mark 16:15 is often referred to as the Great Commission, and I would be remiss, if I did not also state that the words and language used was not merely to make a suggestion, but was actually considered to be equivalent to a military command.

Matthew captured Christ's command in verses 19 and 20 of Chapter 28 this way, "Go therefore and make disciples of all nations, baptizing them in the name of the Father and of the Son and of the Holy Spirit, teaching them to observe all things that I have commanded you, and lo, I am with you always, even to the end of the age." (NKJV) Notice the words "all things that I have commanded you". Past tense. What had He already commanded them? Let's look further:

2. To "Go... Make Disciples" of Jesus is to make them pupils and followers of His. Discipleship can only be performed after evangelism: They went (evangelized) and then they made disciples. Please note evangelism and discipleship was considered to be the primary mission of His apostles and His church. Clearly, Jesus intended the mission of His disciples, and the primary function of His church to be a continuation of His own earthly ministry, which He succinctly stated in Matthew 18:11, Luke 19:10 and John 3:17, to "seek and to save the lost."

3. Jesus proclaimed a multifaceted mission of His, and His church, when He walked into the synagogue, picked up the scroll of Isaiah and read, "The Spirit of the Lord is upon Me, because He has anointed Me to preach the gospel to the poor. He has sent Me to heal the broken-hearted, to proclaim liberty to the captives and recovery of sight to the blind, to set at liberty those who are oppressed, and to proclaim the acceptable year of the Lord." (Luke 4:18-19 NKJV)

   "Preach the gospel to the poor" -- Start where most needed and work up. "Heal the brokenhearted" -- Whether from intolerable shame or overwhelming sorrow, the hearts of men are broken. "Recovering of sight to the blind" -- Jesus realized there were people who were physically, mentally, morally, and spiritually in darkness and needed their sight to be restored. "To set at liberty those who are oppressed" -- Those who were perplexed with the problems of life and imprisoned by fear. "To proclaim the acceptable year of the Lord" -- The actual coming of the Kingdom of God, when the Messiah (Jesus) would deal for all time with the separation between humanity and

God, caused by sin – a primary reference to the Year of Jubilee.

4. God sought His church to worship Him. John 4:23 says, "But the hour cometh, and now is, when true worshippers shall worship the Father in spirit and in truth: for the Father seeketh such to worship him." It is God's desire, and He seeketh such, that all "true worshippers" (His church) would worship Him. The Message gives a broader description of what Jesus was saying in John 4:23, "It's who you are the way you live that count before God. Your worship must engage your spirit in the pursuit of truth. That's the kind of people the Father is out looking for; those who are simply and honestly themselves before Him in their worship. God is sheer 'being' itself – Spirit. Those who worship Him must do it out of their very 'being', their spirits, their true selves, in adoration." (As He shared with the woman at the well, He <u>knew</u> her, and knew <u>exactly</u> who she was.)

This function was to serve as a community of worship and fellowship with others and with Jesus, as He said in Matthew 18:20,

"For where two or three are gathered together in my name, there am I in the midst of them."

His desire for their worship and fellowship expressed His desire to have a true relationship with His church, and our relationship with others of like precious faith, as a testimony to the world. Jesus said it this way, "By this shall all men know that ye are my disciples, if ye have love one to another", which will draw others to worship Him also. God's desire was to establish His church of a people in an environment of worship to express their love to Him and to one another. He described in Mark 12:30 & 31, "And thou shalt love the Lord thy God with all thy heart, and with all thy soul, and with all thy mind, and with all thy strength: this is the first commandment. And the second is like, namely this, Thou shalt love thy neighbor as thyself. There is none other commandment greater than these."

5. Jesus desired that believers (His church) would be developed to perform the works of His ministry. The Apostle Paul explained, "[that] he gave some, apostles, and some, prophets, and some, evangelists, and some, pastors and teachers; for the perfecting of the saints, for the work of the

ministry, for the edifying of the body of Christ:" (Ephesians 4:11 & 12)

One of the functions of His church was to develop ministers who would prepare, strengthen, and equip other believers to carry out the works of His ministries in the body of Christ, and to the world.

6. Part of the ministries in the body of Christ, is to inform, and actually introduce others to "the acceptable year of the Lord", the Kingdom of God. In Matthew 5:13 & 14, Jesus said, "Ye are the salt of the earth, but if the salt have lost his savour, wherewith shall it be salted? It is thenceforth good for nothing, but to be cast out, and to be trodden under feet of men. Ye are the light of the world. A city that is set on an hill cannot be hid."

Jesus was intending His church to be "the salt" in the world to bring seasoning, and good flavor of Jesus and His church to the world. As salt was used as an antiseptic, to draw out the infections that had crept into the communities, and remove the infection of evil, the introduction of the Kingdom of God was to introduce others to the spiritual realm which God reigns over;

through the power and the authority of His Kingdom brought to them through the incarnation of the Son of God, Jesus Christ.

7. Time and space would fill many volumes to recapitulate the things the disciples saw and learned of Jesus over the years they spent with Him, and, without a doubt, He showed them each and every experience in the hope that they would each mimic His every action. In Matthew 13:17, He said to them, "For verily I say unto you, That many prophets and righteous men have desired to see those things which ye see, and have not seen them, and to hear those things which ye hear, and have not heard them."

Certainly, Jesus desired His disciples to duplicate the things they witnessed Him doing, both naturally and supernaturally. In addition, He wanted them to: 1) Go into all the world and preach the gospel, and; 2) make disciples of those they had evangelized; 3) preaching to the poor, healing the brokenhearted, proclaiming liberty to the captives, recovering sight to the blind, and proclaiming the acceptable year of the Lord. Further, 4) He desired them to teach the believers to praise, worship and adore Him; and, 5) to develop the new believers to perform the works of His ministry by maturing each new convert to be a minister; and, to 6) be the salt and light to their world reflecting the spiritual world which God reigns over, while winning the lost and building a body of believers, His church. Then, 7) in Mark 3:35, Jesus described another mission of the church, "For whosoever shall do the will of God, the same is my brother, and my sister, and mother."

Through the spiritual realm of the spirit of God, we have communion and fellowship with the third person of the Trinity, the Holy Spirit of God: the Holy Spirit, also known as the Holy Ghost, Who will lead us and guide us in knowing and understanding the will of God.

In Chapter two let's investigate what that looked like during the first thousand years.

Chapter Two

The Early Years

As we segue into this chapter, let's rehearse where we are today in our society; emerging from a pandemic that has virtually shut down the world, but most importantly, in the context of this book, has reshaped our church services as we knew them. Assembling together in corporate worship in our church buildings, following (for the most part), the same weekly routines that have been established through the traditions of our communities, denominations/fellowships, and leadership preferences, have transitioned into online services using social media venues, and drive-in services. Once again, we are now attempting to reunite our congregations in a central location.

In the previous chapter, Jesus said He would build His church, and then He went about showing the disciples He had called, how His church should function through evangelism, discipleship, preaching, teaching and developing additional ministers.

Certainly the future of the church looked promising as the mission and functions began to take shape, but then the endemic of hatred of Jesus engulfed the pharisaical audience of their region. This culminated in the crucifixion of the Master

Builder of the church, and the displacement of the disciples. Three days later, the resurrection of Jesus Christ brought a renewed energy and fresh vision of their mission to establish His church.

However, now faced with the lingering effects of the endemic, they needed supernatural guidance. Knowing this, Jesus told them to stay in Jerusalem and wait for the "promise of the Father", which they had already heard Him speak of. After the Holy Ghost would come upon them they would receive the supernatural power that they would need to be His witnesses, to spread His gospel to the ends of the earth.

Immediately after He had instructed His disciples to tarry in Jerusalem and wait for the "promise of the Father", Acts 1:9 says, "… He was taken up; and a cloud received Him out of their sight", as He ascended into heaven.

As we look at the progression of His church, following the endemic of their time, may I suggest that we follow suit and tarry with our discipler (Jesus Christ), and with other disciples, as we emerge from our pandemic until we hear God speak to us, "This is the way, walk ye in it."

As the Holy Spirit descended and fell upon those gathered in the Upper Room and endued them with the power and spiritual authority they would need, scripture tells us they departed with "singleness of heart". Following the leading of the Holy Spirit, they performed miracles, through their faith in Christ. Acts, chapter two, tells us that many signs and wonders were performed. There are over twenty miracles specifically mentioned throughout the book of Acts. In addition, the disciples and other apostles were also teachers of the gospel of the Kingdom of God.

I should pause here to remind you that Christianity didn't simply appear with a full set of rules, policies, doctrines and theology. It was slowly developed over the course of the first millennium as the apostles sought the guidance of the Holy Spirit to guide them through the various cultures He led them to and, in essence, changed their civilizations. Nevertheless, the spread of Christianity was influenced more by the cultures, than it influenced the cultures. As Christianity spread, its influence was contingent upon the leaders' (kings, emperors, and other rulers) acceptance, often through their own conversions.

Simply stated, if the leaders of the region where an apostle was endeavoring to start a church did not see and understand the benefit of the church, the resistance would typically result in the failure of the church, and the departure of the apostle(s), shaking the "dust off of their feet" (Luke 9:5).

Far more than the twelve disciples became apostles (from the Greek word apostolos, meaning "messenger"), and the New Testament has only fragmented information about their ventures of spreading the gospel and the persecution they endured.

Nevertheless, tradition indicates that:
1. Peter was killed by Emperor Nero around 64 C.E., crucified and hung head downward, as he had desired.

2. Andrew was martyred by crucifixion in Patras, Greece.

3. James, the brother of John, was put to death by the sword in Jerusalem, about 44 C.E. (Acts 12:1-2).

4. John was exiled from Ephesus to the island of Patmos, survived being boiled in oil, and is believed to have died of old age in 98 C.E. after returning to Ephesus.

5. Philip is thought to have been killed about 80 C.E., although the nature of his death has been much debated.

6. Bartholomew was probably martyred in India, of an extremely cruel death.

7. Matthew was believed to have been martyred around 60 C.E. in Nadabah, Ethiopia while he was teaching in a church. He was nailed to the ground, and beheaded.

8. Thomas was believed to have died in India in 72 C.E., stabbed with spears.

9. James, the brother of Jesus, was thought to have been pushed off the pinnacle of a temple in Egypt.

10. Jude was believed to have been martyred in Syria, although the reliability of this belief has been greatly questioned.

11. Simon the Zealot's death has been presumed to have been in several countries on several various dates. Nevertheless, presumed to have been a martyr's death.

12. Judas Iscariot's death is documented in Matthew 27 and Acts 1. Although the accounts may be somewhat contradictory, we do know he committed suicide soon after betraying Jesus.

13. Matthias, chosen to succeed Judas, has several traditions of death given, with most occurring in Jerusalem at an old age.

Of greatest significance is that these apostles, plus Paul and many others, travelled thousands of miles throughout the then known world of Southern Europe, Asia, what is now Syria, Iran, Iraq, and down to India and Egypt. They brought with them the good news of Jesus Christ and the Kingdom of God to all with whom they encountered: the widows, fatherless, and orphans; feeding the hungry, hurting, and afflicted; healing the sick and raising the dead; and sharing the love that was taught to them by the chief Master Builder, Jesus Christ.

It is obvious by the Gospels, that Matthew, Mark, Luke, and John each took copious notes through the weeks, months, and years they were with Jesus. Later, probably a professional scribe copied their writings, which were afterwards copied multiple times by others, and left at the churches that other itinerant missionaries, mostly called bishops, planted on their journeys, while training others for the ministry of the local church before leaving.

Though not without much rejection and persecution, as time passed, Christianity grew and prospered as it continued to spread across the globe, and was accepted by the communities, and most importantly, by their leaders.

But what about the years that followed? Has much changed in the latter years?

Chapter Three

The Latter Years

Turn the calendar back to the beginning of the 20th Century. The United States was just getting over the long-term effects of the Civil War, which had nearly destroyed our nation. Then, on July 28, 1914, World War I began. Unlike the Civil War, this war was a global war, centered in Europe. Our families were again disrupted.

Now, move the calendar forward about eleven years, after the end of WWI in 1918, somewhere around September 4, 1929 the stock prices began to fall in the United States, and became worldwide news with the stock market crash of October 29, 1929. This period, known as the Great Depression, was a devastating global economic depression that started in most nations in 1930 and lasted through the late 1930's, or mid-1940's, for some nations. Although recovery in the United States began in 1933, our nation did not realize its 1929 Gross National Product levels again for over a decade; in fact, the United States still had an unemployment rate of 15% (plus or minus, in some states in 1940).

After the Civil War, tens of thousands of people were relocated from their homes, in an effort to find employment. After WWI, hundreds of thousands were forced to move to find employment.

The decade-long Great Depression caused well over one million people to move in order to find work.

World War II, the second world war on a global level, which lasted from September 1, 1939 to September 2, 1945, added even more relocations, to an already countless number of moves.

Over the past 100 years an innumerable number of young men, and many young women had made moves across our nation; many travelling great distances. For illustrative purposes, I'll add myself to this mix, having moved as far east as North Carolina, South Carolina and Delaware, as far south as Mississippi, as far north as Pennsylvania and Illinois, and as far west as Texas and Wyoming. My point being, we are a transient people.

Now, consider this, the first time the young man moved, in search of employment, he found a job, felt financially able to support a family, married, and began going to 'her' church. The economy soured, there was a lay-off, and this young family moved again. They were invited by their new neighbors to *First Church*, where the people were friendly, so they connected and stayed. Possibly born a Methodist, raised a Baptist and now a Pentecostal; not to forget the spouse was Lutheran, until her father moved the family and she became a Presbyterian.

May I remind you that George Barna, and others, have been informing us for many years of the erosion of denominational or fellowship loyalty.

That's only on our continent, what about other continents? What's happening?

Christianity began as a sect of Judaism, simply because the Christians were initially all Jews, and was embraced by the Gentiles in its earliest years and by many other ethnicities as the years passed.

According to the Pew Forum, and the Center for the Study of Global Christianity, the number of Christians around the world today has nearly quadrupled in the last 100 years, from about 600 million in 1910 to more than two billion in 2010; the world's population has also nearly quadrupled from approximately 1.8 billion in 1910 to 6.9 billion in 2010, during the same time period. With the percentage of the world's population growth of 285% and the growth of Christianity of 235%, Christians make up approximately the same percentage of the world's population today (32%) as it did a century ago (35%).

To the credit of Christian missionaries, the percentage of Christian population is increasing on every continent, with the exception of Europe, which has declined from over 66% to now under 26%, due in large part by secularism and a loss of confidence in the church. Some would suggest that 26% refers to those having a traditional/cultural affiliation. If the 'Christian' reference was to an evangelical Christ-follower having a redemptive (born again) experience, then Europe's Christian population would be about 3% or less.

So... what does the Christian church look like around the world today?

First, we would all agree that Christian worship involves praising God "in spirit and in truth" in both music, and in speech.

In music: through corporate congregational singing, and through choirs and individuals.

In speech: through scripture readings, teaching and preaching, and through prayer.

Worship in <u>speech</u> is either liturgical (scripted) or non-liturgical (unscripted). Non-liturgical is less 'formal' and provides greater flexibility for the structure of the worship service, and most would agree allows greater focus on the adoration of God. Informal, non-liturgical worship generally also attracts more people. Non-liturgical worship would also include Charismatic worship, which is less structured and more free-flowing than other forms of worship. It has been my experience that a growing number of Evangelical Christians lean more toward this style of worship, where there is a placed emphasis on the person of the Holy Spirit. A Charismatic Christian will often emphasize Jesus' teaching of John 4:24, "God is a spirit, and they that worship him must worship him in spirit and in truth."

Worship in <u>music</u> may also involve other accompaniments such as small bands, large orchestras, blowing a shofar, waving flags, or a form of dancing.

After a few decades of 'Worship Wars'; trying to decide which style of worship was preferred between contemporary, traditional, or a "blend" of both, the pendulum has landed in the unsuspecting position of 'none of the above'. Although there will always be some who prefer strictly contemporary or strictly traditional, by a large degree the 'style' of worship is not the primary concern of most worshippers. Most worshippers simply want genuine, authentic worship with songs that include a deep theological truth with a tempo that resembles praise, and not a somber funeral ritual. They also want to see some forethought and planning in the 'flow' of the worship and not empty spaces where the worship leader, or team, is grasping for the next perfunctory thing to do, say, or sing. They are not looking for a professional worship, but they do want authenticity. After all, the Christian's life is to be an expression of true, authentic worship.

While Jesus Christ is the solid foundation on which the Christian church was founded, we must remember that foundation is immovable and unchangeable.

As Christianity spread across the ancient Middle East, it encountered tension from every culture through which it travelled; through Asia, Europe, Africa, and across to North and South America, and Australia... to the Islands, the mountains and the valleys. Each culture presented a new tension, a different struggle, and a new challenge.

I have been privileged to have travelled in and through over forty countries on five continents, and have ministered in many of those countries, and I can only imagine the struggles the missionaries encountered planting churches, both with language, and culture.

As the world emerges from the Covid-19 Pandemic, it is the belief of many that our cultures will once again change; forever. Accordingly, we will need to readdress the culture inside most of our churches. No, not the foundation of the church, and not the mission of the church, but in the methodologies of how we 'do church'.

In the next chapter, I want to consider some of the changes we might struggle with during our post-pandemic shift. The same struggles many church planters and revitalizers have faced, or others seeking church growth have faced.

I invite you to join me with an open, prayerful, and thoughtful mind and spirit.

Chapter Four

The Next Church

Whether you are planting a new church, revitalizing an existing church, structuring for church growth, or emerging from a global pandemic as we are today, there are some basic elements that must be included in the core values of the mission of our churches:

1. Evangelism;
2. Discipleship;
3. Preaching and teaching the good news of the Kingdom of God;
4. Worship;
5. Leadership and ministry development; and
6. Being "salt" and "light".

The culture of your region will have an influence on what that looks like, and how that's done, but these essentials must be an integral, proactive, part of your ministry.

Additionally, you must have a system or standard of measurement in place, to ensure your methods are providing the results you are seeking. One of those metrics will be your Monday morning staff meetings.

After you celebrate the accomplishments of Sunday's service(s), (salvations, baptisms, rededications, deliverances, and so forth), spend time discussing how the results could have been better. I'm not suggesting personal attacks here, but rather, tweaking what was good, and making it better.

At a minimum, annually, at best quarterly, ask yourself these questions, and be brutally honest.

1. Why does our church exist? Also, why do our ministries (children, youth, young adults, men, women, small groups, seniors, and so forth) exist?

After a period of time many churches fall into a rut; and we all know a rut is simply a grave, with both ends kicked out.

I have observed, and I'm sure you have also at some point somewhere; that the typical church service simply becomes 'routine'. We greet and thank those for coming, open with prayer, and maybe give a couple of announcements. Then, we transition into singing a couple songs, followed by prayer for the sick, and offering, with a couple more songs afterwards. Before the message there may be a couple more announcements. A message (that is oftentimes read, or at least heavily relied upon notes), with a closing prayer, and possibly an invitation for salvation, or something else. <yawn>

Most services are extremely 'predictable'. If yours is not, good for you! Seriously! But many, if not most, are.

There is nothing wrong with having an order of service, however, when our focus is on 'why we exist', there is a spirit of freedom that envelopes who we are and what we are doing, which eliminates the 'status quo' and perfunctory order of the service.

In recognizing why our church exists, do we have goals and objectives for each service; and are those goals and objectives a major part of who we are, and why we exist?

Is the service evangelistic, with an emphasis on salvations? Is the service geared toward strengthening families or marriages? Is it a mission's service to introduce/reintroduce people to the outreaches of the church (at home and abroad)?

Why does our church exist? What are we passionate about, in every ministry of our church?

> 2. Why do people come to our church? Is it because of one, or more, of our ministries?

Our city has more than nine very different grocery stores. Yes, they all sell groceries, but each has their own very unique 'flavor' (pun intended).

Food Lion is a no frills basic store with ordinary food. Aldi has their own brands, primarily; to keep prices low. Harris Teeter has a few more international foods and specialty stuff. Walmart Neighborhood store has additional nonfood items. But Fresh Market, has the best meats, barrels of other specialties, and the best deli counter. Then there's Publix, Lidl, Tropicana and Save-a-Lot, and a couple Mom & Pops'.

Kind of like the churches in your town. So, why do people come to <u>your</u> church?

Is it because of your style of worship? Your location? Your facilities? Other? When you determine what that is, should you add another aisle (figuratively speaking)? Are you capitalizing on your strong points, and making them stronger?

3. Conversely, why don't others come here? (age, ethnicity, gender, other?)

I don't suggest that you change your doctrine or theology. If you are trying to reach a more traditional group, I don't suggest you go all out 'traditional' and eliminate 'contemporary' (maybe blended?).

Maybe your nursery smells, or your facilities need upgrading. What is it, have you intentionally thought about it? Can you make your church more inviting to others, without compromising the gospel?

4. What are other churches in our area (or outside of our area) doing that we are not, and should be?

Some churches have larger staffs, and are able to do more. Some have learned how to recruit (and keep) volunteers to perform the same ministries. Some people/staffs are simply more creative, and love to do what others believe to be impossible. Maybe it's not impossible; maybe you just haven't tried it?

One day the Apostle Peter learned he could walk on water, under the right conditions. There is no limit to what you can do (under the right condition).

Zig Ziglar said: "When obstacles arise, you change your direction to reach your goal; you do not change your decision to get there."

5. Are we actively and consistently training additional leaders in each area of our ministries?

If you want your leaders to do more, expose them to additional opportunities to gain new insights, and encourage them to take someone else 'along for the ride'.

> 6. Which of our ministries is most successful? Why?

There typically seems to be one or two ministries that are more successful than some of the others. Why is that? Is it the personality of the leader(s)? Is it the budget? Is it something that can be replicated with excellence in other ministries?

Note: When attempting to make changes in a new or existing ministry, start small, transition gradually, and examine each step's results carefully before moving on.

> 7. Is there a Mission Statement and a Vision Statement for each of our ministries?

Mission Statements and Vision Statements always help to keep everyone on the same course; and, help to eliminate any confusion about where they are going, and how they want to get there. Some ministries simply flounder because their leaders are not clear on what their mission is, and don't have a short- or long-range vision for the future.

Sit down with each of your ministry leaders and readdress the mission and vision of the ministry with them. If there is no Mission Statement or Vision Statement in writing, help them craft the statements, and then revisit those statements on a regular schedule with them.

8. If there is discord or conflict in any of our ministries, is it handled quickly and appropriately? How?

As sure as the sun will rise tomorrow, there will always be a degree of discord in every group. Clouds may hide the sun, and fake smiles may hide the discord, but trust me, it's there.

Is your ministry team strong enough to be honest and transparent with one another? If not, talk about it openly and honestly. Teach your team the difference between 'constructive criticism' and 'personal attacks'

Handle the issues quickly, and handle them caringly and lovingly.

9. Do we have an effective, proactive, evangelism ministry?

"If you build it, they will come" does not work in ministry. You have spent much time in prayer and planning, and have designed some amazing ministries; but is your community aware of them? Word-of-mouth is always the best form of evangelism, but some people are so introverted that they would rather swallow a live cricket, than invite someone to a church ministry.

Nevertheless, why will they stop everyone and tell them about the exceptional meal they had at 'that' restaurant? Because they fell in love with the meal; it was superb! The server was great, and the ambiance was magnificent.

Is the meal you're serving in your ministries superb (or are you just going through the motions)? Are the servers great, (from the greeters and the ushers to the staff)? Or is everyone just doing their job? How about the ambiance? Does it cry out praise and worship to the God of creation?

If they do, everyone in your church will want to ensure your community knows about it.

Ask yourself, and your staff, "How can we improve our evangelism?" In addition to word-of-mouth, web site, social media, handouts, newspaper articles, what else can we do?

10. Is our 'back door' closed, or at least hard to open?

Do you have 'zone captains' assigned in the sanctuary, and other attended ministries, to follow-up with absentees?

Do you have a plan, such as a phone call, text, email, letter, visit, for first-time, second-time (consecutive), third-time (consecutive) absences?

I once attended a church for <u>years</u>, and had to miss a few consecutive weeks. No one contacted me. Nothing. Nada. Zilch. The back door of that church was wide open, with no door-keepers.

You don't need to smother people, but a simple text message or card that says, "I missed seeing your smiling face on Sunday" will sure encourage the recipient.

> 11. What do our parishioners value most in our ministries? Can that be duplicated in other ministries?

Is your ministry worth the investment of someone's time? Does it add significance to their life? Is it important to them? Some do, some may not. Find those that do, and investigate the reason(s) why and then try to duplicate those things in the other ministries of your church.

If a particular ministry is not adding any value to the parishioners, maybe it time to 'deep-six' it. Some ministries have a particular 'shelf life', and when it's expired, it's time to let it go. You'll know.

12. Are our volunteers shown appreciation and given continuing training?

If you want it done right, you'll have to train them, and continuously train them. If you want them to stay, you'll have to appreciate them, and continuously appreciate them.

It's like the woman who told her husband, "You never tell me you love me"; to which he replied, "I told you I loved you when we got married, and if that ever changes I'll let you know." We all know that just won't work.

Thank you cards, 'Attaboy' from the platform or in the weekly bulletin, appreciation dinners or parties (food works), get to know them and reaffirm their ministry, and check in with them often.

13. Are there new ministries we should start, or old ministries we should revitalize, or for which we should provide an appropriate funeral?

As a church continues to grow there will always be an opportunity for new ministries. Sometimes the 'fresh eyes' of a new parishioner will see the need through a different lens than what others see. The growing church will embrace the opportunity for a new ministry, but a plateaued or declining church will meet new ideas with a rebuttal of, "this is the way we've always done it, and we see no reason to change".

On the other hand sometimes some of the ministries "we have always done this way" need to be revitalized, or, possibly terminated.

It's always difficult to terminate something that's been around forever, but there comes a time when we need to just move on. Put each of your ministries under a microscope and ask yourself, is this still producing the results we're looking for? If not, celebrate the past results of that ministry, and announce its termination.

> 14. What ministries and/or events provide the highest benefits/results for our church?

There are some ministry events that most churches see high benefits, such as Easter and Christmas Cantatas. If promoted properly, and at the time of the event if you have captured follow-up information, and actually follow-up with those people, you will no doubt add folks to your attendance, and better yet, add names in the Lamb's Book of Life. Nevertheless, I have seen some churches that capture the follow-up information, file it away, and do nothing with it.

Examine the ministries of your church, to include Small Group ministries, and ask yourself if they are providing the results you're expecting.

Look at the other annual events on holidays, and evaluate if those events are beneficial.

> 15. Which event(s) is/are least profitable and not good stewardship of our investments (manpower, money, materials)?

I recently spoke with a pastor who had spent thousands of dollars purchasing Easter eggs, and candy for inside them, and then spent an exorbitant amount to have them thrown out of a helicopter onto the church grounds. They also had dozens of people stuffing the eggs, and cleaning the grounds afterwards. The pastor admitted, in the years they had done this, he is not aware of any growth as a result. Manpower, money, and materials and no positive results. Is that good stewardship?

> 16. Do we value people's time with appropriate service/meetings times (including shift workers), and appropriate length for services/meetings?

If attendance has increased, and you need to start another service will you start an earlier service? That is generally the practice. If you have a manufacturing plant or other factory in the area, a hospital, nursing home, retail stores or restaurants that have shift workers, you may want to consider another day, or another time, which would be better for your shift workers. Yes, I realize the challenges with a Tuesday evening or a Thursday morning service, but I have also learned that "God will make a way, where there seems to be no way. He works in ways we cannot see, He will make a way for me...".

Not wanting to stifle the work of the Holy Spirit, let me ask you, "Can you limit your two hour service to an hour and fifteen minutes?" People's attention spans today are not as long as they used to be; and, longer is not necessarily holier.

17. Would a 'satellite' location help us?

Something as simple as having a Christian Education class at a town meeting room, or back room of a restaurant, if we've run out of rooms, or as large as converting a warehouse room into a satellite sanctuary may encourage growth.

Several years ago, at a church I was pastoring, we were experiencing growth, and ran out of Sunday school classrooms. It was suggested to start a class in the McDonalds across the street. As you can imagine there were a lot of curious spectators, and that class ended up being our largest and fastest growing.

Satellite sanctuaries across town of large cities, or in neighboring towns are also seeing great results today; they are more convenient for people, and less financial cost to the church.

Sometimes creativity is the answer.

18. Incidentally, are all of our facilities well maintained and clean, inside and out?

Are our rooms sanitized after every use? Are our restrooms clean and fresh smelling? Is the nursery clean and fresh smelling? Women simply will not overlook a smelly restroom, and certainly do not want their babies in an unclean nursery, playing with toys that have been in the mouths of other children. If you want to attract young families, you must make these areas a priority in cleanliness; particularly in this post-pandemic world we are now living in.

19. Just as Jesus had His disciples to assist Him, do we have a staff (paid or volunteers) to assist us, who are trained and shown appreciation?

There is the old cliché that if you want something done right, you have to do it yourself; and, of course, that is just not true. There are some churches where the pastor does everything: cleans the church, mows the lawn, shovels the snow, and the list goes on, with non-ministerial duties. If you are one of those pastors, shame on you. Please let other people help you. Maybe the only reason they are not, is because you haven't asked them. Ask them, train them, and appreciate them, and you will have a happy helper.

> 20. Would restructuring our staff (paid or volunteers) provide better results?

Do you have a super guy, or gal, on your staff that is just not getting the results you want? You've trained them, appreciated them, and done everything you know to do, but the results are just not there. Maybe that person is merely not in the right position; maybe they are better suited for another position in the church. Paid or volunteer, doesn't really matter; can they trade positions with someone else, or would their talents be better used in another ministry? If possible try an 'experiment' for thirty or ninety days. Give an easy on ramp and off ramp; you may be pleasingly surprised.

> 21. Would paid advertising maximize our attendance for services? For events, or other ministries?

It has been my experience that assistant editors of local newspapers love to help their area's churches. We used to put stories in our paper of what different groups in the church did: cleaned up the city park, painted (with permission) a city owned abandoned warehouse, or cleaned out a culvert that the city workers constantly overlooked. The paper's stories always included pictures of the project, and pictures of the group, with names of the people, and, of course the name and address of the church. Every month we got some seriously great publicity for our church; and, when it came time for a paid ad to publicize an event, we generally got a great discount.

On the other hand, maybe you just need to place some paid ads in the paper for additional exposure of a new ministry, or a special event. If so, ask the paper personnel which day of the week would be best for you, and which section of the paper will work better, and (watch this) rather the ad should be on the top or the bottom of the page. You may be surprised at their suggestions.

> 22. Do we capture the names, addresses, phone numbers and email addresses for each guest/visitor?

Most churches have visitor cards they have used since Moses was a corporal. You run out, and just have more printed. But when was the last time you looked at the cards? Do they capture all the information you need? When you are welcoming your guests, do you explain your purpose for the cards, to keep them informed of special events? Do you also mention that if they are uncomfortable with completing any portion of the card they can just leave that portion blank? Otherwise you may not get a card at all. Some people just don't want to give their email address or phone number (they already get enough spam); and some people don't want to share what year they were born, but the month and date are okay. Be flexible.

Also, most people don't mind a follow-up email or text message, but cold visits and phone calls are generally not appreciated. Know the area's culture where you are, and respect it.

> 23. Do we also capture their childrens' names and ages, or birthdates?

They are a part of the family also, and they like to know they are included. Many families go to a church because their children first wanted to. Don't neglect them.

> 24. Do our children's and youth ministry leaders send separate correspondence to their children and youth?

What child or youth doesn't like getting a text message? What child or youth doesn't enjoy getting a birthday card? If you hook the child, you will typically hook the parents.

> 25. Is our web site and Facebook page kept up to date with useful, fresh, and inviting information?

If not, do you have a tech-savvy person in your church that would do this (with your guidance, of course)?

How many times have you Googled a business, or maybe a church, only to realize their web site was still advertising the Christmas play from eight months ago, or their Facebook page had not had an entry for months.

If your social media sights are out of date, it will be presumed that the rest of your church is also out of date. People today get their first impression of something from the internet; make it a great first impression.

Seotribunal.com says there were over 5 billion Google searches per day in 2018. That's 1.825 trillion per year, and the average person contributes 3 or 4 a day to that total. Please, do not underestimate the value of your web site or Facebook page. People can use your web site to sign up for an event, or even to conveniently pay their tithes, and a host of other things.

> 26. What are people in our church saying to the people in our community about our church?

No doubt they're saying something, but what are they saying? At the end of your message make a simple comment: "If you've heard something today that has encouraged you, tell others this week as you get the chance. We want them to be encouraged also". Give people an opportunity to tell others something good about the church they attend, and they will invite more people to join them.

> 27. What are the people in our community saying about our church?

Ask a stranger at the grocery store, "What do you know about [insert your church name here]?" Ask several people that question and, if you get 'caught' invite them to church. You may have just met one of your new Small Groups leaders.

> 28. Is our church outward focused, assisting our community?
>
>> Are we routinely asking our mayor or town/city council how our church, or groups in our church, could bless our community?

If you are not already doing this, make it a priority; it will give your church the favorable publicity you are looking for, and need.

On the Fourth of July do you have a special service to honor, and thank, the leaders of your community? It's a great time to invite your city/town leaders, your county (or parish); city council members and state representatives, fire fighters and police. Let them know you pray for them, and drop by their offices with a box of donuts periodically. Reach out to your community.

29. Are we proactively blessing the missionaries our church supports?

Do they frequently receive cards from you for their birthdays (for each family member) and anniversary?

When you have a mission's service do you Facetime or Skype them on the platform screen?

They are away from home, and away from much of their family for years at a time, and when they're home they are busy itinerating and raising support, that they don't have much time to be with their family. Look for ways to bless them.

30. What are our three biggest obstacles, and how can we correct or eliminate them?

Those obstacles may be people, finances or facilities, and an obstacle in one ministry may be very different from an obstacle in another ministry. Are you taking the time with your ministry leaders to be able to understand what obstacles they are struggling with?

31. What are our three biggest blessings, and how can we capitalize on them?

Blessings come in all shapes and sizes. The important thing is to recognize them, celebrate them, and extend those blessings as far as possible.

> 32. What are our two-year, five-year, and ten-year plans, and what are we doing to prepare for and meet those goals?

Do you have future goals for your ministries? Are you preparing to split ministries into subgroups? If you take one mission's trip a year, are you preparing to take one a quarter or, one a month? Does everyone on your ministry team share the same goals? Do you have incremental plans for reaching those goals?

> 33. If we could change just one thing, what would we do?

I would venture to say everyone would like to change something. Is your 'something' significant, or trivial? What's holding you back?

Not every mountain is worth dying for, and not everything needs to be changed. Sometimes just our perception of the issue needs to be changed, and, yes, sometimes somethings DO need to be changed.

If you are confronted with one of those things that you know needs to be changed, then, why don't you just do it? (Even Jesus overturned the moneychanger's table.)

> 34. Once again, said another way: Should anything be added, deleted, simplified, or changed in some other way?

You can't do the same thing over and over, and expect a different result. Albert Einstein said that's the definition of insanity. If you are looking for a different result, then you probably need to add something, delete something, or change something. What is it?

> 35. As a result of this meeting, what is going to be done, who is going to do it, and what is the suspense time/date for its completion?

You can have this meeting once a year, or once a quarter, or, even once a month, but if you never decide what will be done, who will do it, and when it will be done... guess what? Nothing will be done, and you will continue to get the same results you have always gotten; or, worse yet, your attendance will continue to decline.

Jesus was very organized in laying the foundation of His church, and extremely methodical and intentional in the process (since the beginning of time). Shouldn't we be also?

I am eagerly waiting to hear the Master Church Builder one day say to me, "Well done thou good and faithful servant."

Whether you are a church planter, revitalizer, striving to emerge from a pandemic or endemic, or just laboring for church growth, I pray this book has been, and will continue to be a blessing to you, your family, and your ministry.

Ray James

Chapter Five

A Post-Pandemic Word

For 99.9% of us, there has never been a more difficult time for the church, and time for His Church, in our lifetime.

Anxieties are rising every day. Frustrations are mounting seemingly with every attempt to make sense of what is happening in our world, in our town, and even, for many, in our families.

Despair has taken on a new meaning for many people, and for many people fear is invading nearly every hour of every day, in some form.

Will things ever return to normal? If not, what will the new normal look like?

If your church is open again, and you had extremely high expectations for attendance, based on the number of people following your live-streaming services, but your attendance is actually only a fraction of the pre-pandemic numbers, are you wondering what's going on with that?

Maybe your finances have fallen to a point that you can no longer manage to pay your bills, and you are literally losing sleep over it.

May I encourage you with a few scriptural truths?

First, please remember you are still a child of God, and He feels your hurt, and He knows your needs; and He has not forsaken you. There are over

100 verses woven throughout the Bible that tells us God is with us, and will not leave us. Over 100, wow! Wouldn't you agree He must want us to know that? Google them, and read them; but most importantly understand the truth in those scriptures.

Understand you are not in this alone, and stay in contact with those in your circle of friends who will encourage you; and, in return, offer your friends words of encouragement. Be a Jonathan to David.

Trust in what you know to be true. God loves you, and has a plan for you, and He has a plan for your church, His church. Jeremiah 29:11 (NLT) says, "For I know the plans I have for you," says the Lord. "They are plans for good and not for disaster, to give you a future and a hope."

"Good and not for disaster", "a future and a hope". Many today are looking for hope. Here it is, embrace it.

Often I have to pause and remember God's words of Isaiah 55:8-9: "For my thoughts are not your thoughts, neither are your ways my ways, saith the Lord. For as the heavens are higher than the earth, so are my ways higher than your ways, and my thoughts than your thoughts."

Don't give up on God; He has not given up on you.

It's interesting, and sometimes amusing to see what people are saying on Twitter, Facebook, or their blogs about what they think God is doing in the world today through this pandemic. Some of their comments are thought provoking, but most of them are plum preposterous.

Who am I to think I know what God is doing? But what I do know is: God is still in total and perfect control of all things, and He's got this!

Not to mention, every day we are one day closer to the Rapture of His Church.

So don't do anything goofy. Stay in touch with the One Who is the Truth, and keep your trust in Him.

I may not have any of the answers, but I know in Whom I have believed, and I am persuaded that He is able to keep that which I've committed, unto Him against that day.

Only God can part the Red Sea waters of this Covid-19 pandemic.

Ray James

Chapter Six

Closing Thoughts

    I long for the atmosphere of the church I knew half a century ago, when I was a little boy; where every week the lost were saved, healings and miracles were witnessed, and the church family was exactly that... one big happy family, and growing every week.

    Regrettably, with very few exceptions, the Church of Jesus Christ has lost the dunamis power and functionality we read about in the Book of Acts, and witnessed in the 1940's and 1950's.

    If the church is going to regain her effectiveness in reaching the lost, and bringing them to the saving knowledge of our Lord and Savior, Jesus Christ, then we must be willing to take a hard look as Christians at: who we are; Whose we are; what we have been called to do; who we have been called to be; and what we need to change, in order to correct our ineffectiveness of the levels we should be reaching; and possibly, our lethargy.

    While pastoring over the past few decades, I have watched churches nearly destroy themselves over issues, which I believe, had simple fixes, and should have never reached the intensities that they did. (You know some of them: "Which version of the Bible should we use?"; "Which style of worship will we have?"; "Will we allow drums?"; "guitars?"; "Why do we need choruses on the wall?" and, "Who took the hymnals?")

No longer is the pastor trying to replace the organ with a piano, by moving the piano across the platform (one inch at a time) until the organ is gone. Now, oftentimes, the piano and the organ are both gone, and we have digital keyboards and other instruments.

In some places, the pastor doesn't even wear a coat and tie anymore, or he doesn't even tuck in his shirt tail. Sister Lovebubble would turn over in her grave, if she saw this.

Without a doubt there are still issues in many churches today, and many of those issues will never be changed to everyone's satisfaction.

So, may I make a suggestion? When you are planting a church, or revitalizing an existing church, or, when you are trying to emerge from the Covid-19 Pandemic, or simply achieve additional church growth, consider the following: Will you humbly let those around you know that you are just trying to please God, and follow the guidance of the Holy Spirit, to win the lost, and protect them from an eternal fiery hell by any means possible, while there is still time? And ask everyone to set aside their petty differences, and join you in taking back everything Satan has robbed from the Church of Jesus Christ.

I'm not for you, and I'm not against you, I'm simply trying to do my very best to be obedient to what I believe God is calling me to do. Will you join me?

Together, we can populate the Kingdom of Heaven; by snatching people out of the clutches of the devil, and eternal damnation; and giving them the opportunity to place their faith in a loving God, Who sent His Son to die for them, so they won't have to die a second death.

One day a King died for me. Incredible!
Abundant blessings !!!

Ray James